For a Wonderful Husband

Smithsonian American Art Museum

HYLAS
PUBLISHING

www.hylaspublishing.com

HYLAS
PUBLISHING

Hylas Publishing
Publisher: Sean Moore
Creative Director: Karen Prince
Production Consultant: Madeleine Day
Designer: Gus Yoo

First published by
Hylas Publishing
129 Main Street, Irvington,
New York 10533
www.hylaspublishing.com

First American Edition published in 2003
02 03 04 05 10 9 8 7 6 5 4 3 2 1

ISBN 1-59258-035-1

Set in Berkley and Goudy
Printed and bound in England by Butler and Tanner
Color origination by Radstock Reproductions Ltd,
Midsomer Norton

Distributed by St. Martin's Press

On the next page you can personalize this book by adding a photograph of your choice, and a message.

"Love conquers
all things:
let us too
give in to love."
Virgil (70-19 BC)

"You know

very well that love is,

above all,

the gift of oneself!"

'Ardele'

Jean Anouilh

(1910-1987)

13

"There is only one
happiness in life,
to love and be loved."
George Sand
(1804-1876)

W. Glackens

"Only the soul
that loves is happy."
'Egment'
Johann Wolfgang von
Goethe (1749-1832)

"If ever two were one, then surely we.

If ever man were loved by wife, then thee;

If ever wife was happy in a man,

Compare with me ye women if you can.

I prize thy love more than whole mines of gold,

Or all the riches that the East doth hold.

My love is such that rivers cannot quench,

Nor ought but love from thee give recompense.

The love is such I can no way repay;

The heavens reward thee manifold, I pray.

Then while we live, in love let's so persever,

That when we live no more we may live ever."

'To My Dear and Loving Husband'

Anne Bradstreet (1612-1672)

"The course
of true love
never did run
smooth."
Proverb

"Who, of men, can tell

That flowers would bloom, or that green fruit would swell

To melting pulp, that fish would have bright mail,

The earth its dower of river, wood and vale,

The meadows runnels, runnels pebble-stones,

The seed its harvest, or the lute its tones,

Tones ravishment, or ravishment its sweet,

If human souls did never kiss and greet?"

'Endymion'

John Keats (1795-1821)

"I get no kick from champagne,

Mere alcohol doesn't thrill me at all,

So tell me why should it be true

That I get a kick out of you?"

'I Get a Kick Out of You'

Cole Porter (1891-1964)

"Then spoke Yajnavalkya:

In truth it is not for the love of a husband

that a husband is dear;

but for the love of Soul in the husband

that a husband is dear.

It is not for love of wife

that a wife is dear;

but for the love of Soul in the wife

that a wife is dear."

Upanishads

"Difficult or easy,
pleasant or bitter,
you are
the same you:
I cannot live
with you
-or without you."
Martial
(AD 40-104)

"I'll love you, dear, I'll love you

Till China and Africa meet

And the river jumps over the mountain

And the salmon sing in the street,

I'll love you till the ocean

Is folded and hung up to dry

And the seven stars go squawking

Like geese about the sky."

'As I Walked Out One Evening'

W.H. Auden (1907-1973)

"It has been said,
that heart speaks
to heart,
whereas language
only speaks to the ears."

St. Francis de Sales

(1567-1622)

"Will you still need me,

will you still feed me,

When I'm sixty-four?"

'When I'm Sixty-Four'

The Beatles

"I know not if I know what true love is,
But I know, then, if I love not him,
I know there is none other I can love."
'Lancelot and Elaine'
Alfred, Lord Tennyson (1809-1892)

"Never pain to tell thy love

Love that never told can be;

For the gentle wind does move

Silently, invisibly."

William Blake (1757-1827)

"If love were what a rose is,

And I were like the leaf,

Our lives would grow together

In sad or singing weather,

Blown fields or flowerful closes,

Green pleasure or grey grief."

'A Match'

Algernon Charles Swinburne (1837-1909)

"Give me a thousand kisses,

then a hundred,

then another thousand,

then a second hundred,

then yet another thousand,

then a hundred."

'Carmina'

Catullus (84-54 BC)

"And they lived
happily ever after."
Anon.

"Women deprived of
the company of men pine,
men deprived of
the company of women
become stupid."

'Notebooks'

Anton Chekhov (1860-1904)

"Love, all alike,
no season knows,
nor clime
Nor hours, days, months,
which are the rags of time."

'The Sun Rising'

John Donne (1572-1631)

"Even quarrels with ones husband are preferable to the ennui of a solitary existence."

-Elizabeth Patterson Bonaparte (1785-1879)

"O that 'twere possible

After long grief and pain

To find the arms of my true love

Round me once again!"

'Maud'

Alfred, Lord Tennyson (1809-1892)

"Chains do not hold
a marriage together.
It is threads,
hundreds of tiny threads
which sew people together
through the years."
Simone Signoret (1921-1985)

"How do I love thee? Let me count the ways.

I love thee to the depth and breadth and height

My soul can reach, when feeling out of sight

For the ends of Being and ideal Grace.

I love thee to the level of everyday's

Most quiet need, by sun and candlelight.

I love thee freely, as men strive for Right;

I love thee purely, as they turn from Praise.

I love thee with a passion put to use

In my old griefs, and with my childhood's faith.

I love thee with a love I seemed to lose

With my lost saints-I love thee with the breath,

Smiles, tears, of all my life!-and, if God choose,

I shall love thee better after death."

'Sonnets from the Portuguese'

Elizabeth Barrett Browning (1806-1861)

"I married my husband
for life, not for lunch."

Unknown

"There may be a little
trouble ahead,
But while there's
moonlight and music
and love and romance,
Let's face the music
and dance."
'Follow the Fleet'
Irving Berlin (1888-1989)

"I'll love you, dear, I'll love you

Till China and Africa meet

And the river jumps over the mountain

And the salmon sing in the street,

I'll love you till the ocean

Is folded and hung up to dry

And the seven stars go squawking

Like geese about the sky."

'As I Walked Out One Evening'

W.H. Auden (1907-1973)

"Stand by your man."

'Stand by Your Man'

Tammy Wynette

(1942-1998)

"He married me with a ring,

a ring of bright water

Whose ripples spread from

the heart of the sea,

He married me with a ring

of light, the glitter

Broadcast on the swift river."

'The Marriage of Psyche'

Kathleen Raine (1908-)

27  28 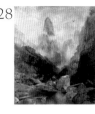 29  30

31 32  33

Picture Credits

All images are from The Smithsonian American Art Museum